Courting Katie

JAMES O'SULLIVAN

Published in 2017 by
Salmon Poetry
Cliffs of Moher, County Clare, Ireland
Website: www.salmonpoetry.com
Email: info@salmonpoetry.com

ISBN 978-1-910669-85-3

COVER IMAGE: *Mary Galvin*
COVER DESIGN & TYPESETTING: *Siobhán Hutson*

Printed in Ireland by Sprint Print

*Salmon Poetry gratefully acknowledges the support of
The Arts Council / An Chomhairle Ealaoín*

For Jonathan

Acknowledgements

An earlier iteration of this manuscript received a High Commendation in the Munster Literature Centre's Fool for Poetry 2014 International Chapbook Competition. "The Holy Ground" was shortlisted for the Fish Poetry Prize 2015.

"Silent Places" has been previously published in *New Eyes on the Great Book*, while "Eyre Square" and "The Laundry" appeared in *The Bohemyth* and *Cyphers*, respectively.

I would like to acknowledge Salmon's wonderful Jessie Lendennie and Siobhán Huston for all of their efforts in making this collection a reality.

My sincerest thanks to Mary Galvin, Graham Allen, Órla Murphy, Paul Casey, and Pat Cotter for supporting my writing in numerous ways and at various junctures.

Thanks to Katie Ahern, whose stories over coffee in the O'Rahilly Building gave rise to a portion of "Free Gaff", and to Mike Waldron and Shane Lordan, whose exhibition at the Crawford Art Gallery has inspired and lent its name to "Visions of Tragedy".

I am also indebted to Christopher Walker, who, without knowing me all that well, offered to give this manuscript its first critique. Both he and Annie are sorely missed now that I have moved on from central Pennsylvania.

Invites to read have always been appreciated, particularly those from the Cork Spring Poetry Festival, Ó Bhéal, the Irish Writers' Centre, and the Canadian Federation for the Humanities and Social Sciences.

Contents

"Your new millennial tiles are cool
beneath the feet of floodlit winter shoppers.
Have you forgotten so quickly
how everything within you burned?"

"Patrick's Street"
GRAHAM ALLEN

The Angels' Share

My baptism had been in a porcelain tub—
in vomit and spit, I tried to keep the session alive—
fuck your Union Jack, we want our country back—
that was a long night, the smell of Paddy
on my hooped shirt, *just like the older boys*—

Nights like these made us hard, well used to retching
as we slept in our bodily stew—cans of cider
still taste like stolen nights spent on bridges,
crowdsourcing fantasy—we got used to the cold,
whiskey and fear kept us warm—we were angels.

Mason Jars

We'd stagger from the library, tenners clutched—
three pints of Beamish that was, *none of the Protestant shit!*
It was always talk of gadgets and Galaxies,
the straggler off dementing women with cards and bollocks—

What use would be our tenners now? Where would we even sit
amongst the poets gathered in filthy hovels eating six-quid-cereal?

We would come up Barrack Street, mocking Mamie and her needles,
though she'd fix our zips and turn our legs for the price of a Redbreast—
She's gone now, the history of her decrepit place put to good use
for commerce—the greasy newspapers, the lessons learned, long gone.

The Burning Cathedral

She told me about growing up in Longford,
in that small house beneath Saint Mel's—
he had always lived in the shadow of that church—
On Christmas Day that shadow rose, black and high,
letting some sun through to touch the crammed houses—
if only he had lived to see it, he'd have died happy—
Letters were penned, coppers were rubbed—
and just as the children crept from their doorways,
the shadow returned.

Katie

I met Katie down on Pana, a young beur
with legs that gave her the walk of a queen—
we shifted off Daunt's Square, where
I told her how she'd blossomed, bloomed,
how there'd never be a man to take my place.

Knocking back Jameson in the Bróg,
we scoffed that we were well beyond places
like this, that the old women passing by
were better suited to the church-like
benches than young boys and girls like us.

Come away, she coaxed, and I did,
down Parnell Place, holding her hair
while she vomited, my left foot lodged
in discarded pizza, the smell of urine
in my nostrils, ready to be held myself.

Eyre Square

Crystal chimes with the vibrations from the guests overhead,
but if you complain it shows a terrible lack of sophistication,
that you aren't used to the clang of a sensitive chandelier.

Heavy curtains conceal tall windows, protected out the front,
but backed up by newer stuff that slides the opposite way,
so you can open the old and new at once, to let the air in.

The view is of the Square, a view enjoyed by Dev himself,
and Lemass, Fitzgerald, Dalglish, even Charles de Gaulle.
It was taken and put to use by Her Majesty's Forces once,

before our dealings saw it returned, and promptly handed over
to one of Ireland's many armies, who lost and won it back.
It suffered the Emergency, but enjoyed a boom from the railways.

Liam O'Flaherty sat there for much of the renaissance, straining
for the echoes of voices. Do the same, and you'll note the drunks
pissing on the pathway, stumbling along in the name of Patrick.

Outbound

Barrack Street was your last port of call
before you went to pick olives in Darwin—
a final burger, plain, with a splash of chips
that I didn't dare touch until you offered.
You were crying because you had to leave
some girl whose name I hadn't heard before,
not like when every word had come from me.
I put just one arm around you, like a man does,
and told you to savour every moment of it—
if short a few bob, you knew where I was.
And in that brief moment, we didn't think
on adventures, or economies, or ministers,
or when we might see each other again—
but of hanging off the edge of bunks,
arguing about Ferguson and Wenger,
chatting about teachers, mischief, and girls.

Those Streets

Those streets are where I bled, I'd say,
smashed against some wall by Dave,
the big fucker, good at *the oval ball*
back then, like all the fat lads—
put them to rugby or stick them in goals.
The fucking fishing and chips, I'd say,
lashings of salt and vinegar,
mushy peas and curry,
I used go for the breast supper,
like my mam, she's on the southern fry now—
she'd turn tricks for chicken.
Those streets are where I had my first shift,
some young wan in the Vic,
a den for drugs and predators I'd explain,
like there was something dangerous
in machines that would steal your twenty pee.
Those streets are where I'd neck naggins,
where the mist would be worth the warm glow
of candlelight in some snug, stout waiting
on a table, *scratched to fuck*,
every step with meaning, some memory.
They'd watch me with resigned faces,
trading glances as I talked of Neverland.
And I'd rise in the mornings
to venture through the marble halls,
greeting the deans and professors,
dangling measured words until they'd ask—
Me? I'm from fucking Cork, boy!

Remote

When you left,
I knew everything
had changed—
there were fewer
discarded mega-deals,
and less casualties
in the war
for the remote.
I wanted to be
your little
older brother again,
troubled by videogames
and football shirts,
feeling entirely different
about tomorrow.

The Laundry

It was by the greasy spoon,
a half-mile from the Lough,
a few doors down from Ryan's—
my mother would send
me along with plastic bags
when she hadn't the time,
or the washing machine
was on the blink, *leaking again*.
It was close to my grandmother's,
so I'd pop in there for tea;
listen to stories
while she did her needle work,
before heading back
to collect a bundle of sheets
rinsed so thoroughly
you could wrap the Baby Jesus in them.
It was work for fallen women once,
but that's a story from way back when;
there's few old enough to tell it right,
if any left at all.
Packie Bonner's save,
now you'll hear that if you want it,
from Italia 90—
a tale that benefits
from being within living memory.
That was the year
they found Caravaggio's masterpiece,
The Taking of Christ,
hanging in the Jesuit hold
on Lower Leeson Street,
the same road Gerry Ryan
called home before he died—
a sad day that,
it had everyone talking.
It was always a spot for meeting
the most notable fellas,

literary and business types,
the sort that wouldn't waste time
with Apache Chiefs,
and would know
how to appreciate such fine work.
It would have been clearer
with a few more lanterns,
but the polished surface
of the arresting officer's arm
offers light enough—
it has been thoroughly scrubbed,
so as to ensure it does not go unnoticed
when spotted amongst the bustle
of a modern European capital.

The Home

Sent to the abbeys,
their children slept in cages—
lying emaciated,
boils on their bodies—
"It is not here
that we must look
for cause of death."
These jailors took care;
it must have been
a pylon or a mast—
They grew,
and left their cages,
to die in their homes,
lying emaciated,
boils on their bodies—

Silent Places

There is a park in Nara, where rust and grime
are all that greet the fog as it rolls through
this forgotten place, and a city in northern Ukraine,
long remembered, that is just as silent but for
the squeal of fluorescent iron twisting in the wind.

We know of the sheds in Wexford, but deep
in finer constructs, there are ghosts kept locked
behind two-inch Plexiglas, fading slightly as the air
seeps into their silent necropolis—but it is safe here,
in solitude, where their labours will not be in vain.

Look out across this wasteland—the Burren
has spread, making Nara and Pripyat of Togher
and the Lough—there are no benefactors at hand
to save the young philistines queuing at Cork Airport—
and now, as the fog rolls in, here too, it greets silence.

Necropolis

You could hardly think when the wind swept
over that tin roof—a shed converted to a bedroom—
rattling in the night, with stray drops on the sheets,
from the ceiling, jarring you awake as something
scratched at plasterboard, desperate to make it
to the other side, beyond the falling sea.

A plastic lamp of seemingly perpetual light
casts a shadow on the pack of lickspittles—
did you know then that he'd be your patron?
You'd grope for structure here too, where mushrooms
grow in the sill, but don't know which way to reach—
did the bailout from Ulster Bank help *your* groping?

There was more sweat than craft poured here,
and nights spent sleeping, with muscles sore
from cutting into Kingspan with a handsaw.
Are these inadequacies made lesser by seven-figure
tomes, locked away? Here is your necropolis,
in this basement, where words come to die.

American Telly

We're well used to folly, to adopting, pell-mell,
the half-baked produce of a larger tyrant
that snuck in without laying a violent hand.

We've been told what we must do to produce
our best, to resist the solemn-eyed; keep our heads
above the gushing waters, and dim sands.

But, when he asks if she wants to go 'round again,
and they thank us at the end for the ride, you see
what you have to fear—and you adore every moment.

The Holy Ground

It greets you like a bookshelf, or the selection
in a sweetshop—Saint Colman keeping a watchful
eye on greedy little boys, and mischievous girls,
reaching for a taste of something sharp and sour—
Black Jacks and Fruit Salads—gobbled all at once,
packed and chewed between watery cheeks.

Joseph guards the western door, so children
might not pass with sticky fingers, smudging
the fine limestone from Mallow, the blue
Dalkey granite and Kilkenny marble,
the Belgian slate, and Californian pitchpine.
Here is not a place for unwashed children.

Sailors sang about this oasis, raising anchors,
hoping to find a torn rigging that might send them
for shore with the secrets of their mind piled high.
Vigil is still kept from the hill, but like the shanties,
they have been seen for what they are—the shop fronts
are fading now, and children keep hold of their mothers.

Ghost Towns

An old forgotten Ford leans on tireless rims,
sockets bulging from where its eyes were gouged,
its face wilting, frozen in time. It's some model
only the keenest of connoisseurs could now discern,
its spokes digging into parched Nevada floor.

In Limousin, there is a graveyard for these,
a martyred village where rust reigns over man's
discarded toys, buried beneath the crumbling
walls and scorched bricks. The sun casts hideous
shadows over the skeletons of bedroom furniture.

They say we don't have any, but for a cardboard set,
now gone, that sprung up on the Dingle peninsula—
there are more of these, pockmarks where echoes
rattle among the thin walls and brown swing sets
on ground as parched and scorched as anywhere.

Fadó Fadó

Memory suggests that things were simpler
back when waxy green leaves were money—
If you stumbled on a chance lash of hazel
you could command armies—conquer worlds.

You're not long a conqueror—branches
make way for Panini stickers,
real jerseys, white boots, and Puffin books,
piled for admiration on your neighbour's desk.

Fadó fadó—always with the turn of tongue
that hints at fonder times, when penny sweets
and Tayto sandwiches filled excited bellies
before dawn convoys to Ireland's coliseum.

There was always a rush for sausage rolls
and Dunkin' Donuts, the same onlookers
fixed on warriors contesting their prize, paying
little heed to the cries of the mob—ass, ass!

Sovereign rings of the finest sterling silver
adorned the hands of natives—renegades
painted in green and white hoops, singing
in fields on the eve of Old Firm derbies.

On Graball there was a hooded crow,
perched on a rood of barnacled rock
that nobody wanted because of the way
it faced—the other crows calling him grey.

Shopping Centre

They wore uniforms
like only young boys know.
"The difference," he explained,
"is that mine is just tan."

The Sea

i

Three days he lay in a corridor,
strangers passing
on their phones,
getting the latest from Corrie.
The Bishop came and blessed him,
before retiring to the stoic life,
crossing the Grand Parade
where noble students took the day to collect
the salaries of non-profit tycoons
and their cohorts.
We put in lights
and turn them off to keep jobs
for the boys—
just like it is in the towers and quads.
Messy Monday they called it,
when children were trampled
for the sake of cheap shots.

ii

She told me to only write
when I felt it get caught in my throat—
if I had to force any bit,
then it would never work.
And I told myself to read
so I might learn to be better,
but there is nothing to be gained
when others have said it all,
when they have described this sea as it is,
in perfect phrasing.

Across the Divide

I met them coming across Craigavon,
their clothes ragged from the years of toil—
set before the paler sky, their gesture seemed clear.

I sat with them for a while—we didn't speak—

Rattling pebbles against the wall,
my eyes turned to that limp wrist—
was that a hand that wanted taking?
And that face, that face so empty,
what was that face, its gaze cast down?
It seemed to me a face that longed to look
upon a lover lost, a beaten face, without scars—
not that kind of beating, the deeper kind,
that is never raw, but forever casts a dull ache.
The hand before was not what it sought—
it might as well have been clutching at death,
that face, so sad. Empty, lost, and sad.

The other wrist was straight and stern—
this was the hand that was doing the taking.
That face, that was sure—of itself, its purpose, its right.

Beyond my friends was a picture,
from a childhood storybook, I think it came—
the Bogside, and the Fountain—
megaphones, berets, sledgehammers—
and that yellow hand, the surest hand.
It's all in the past that, forgotten now.
And yet, I see a Sky satellite dish, a clothes horse,
toys strewn across a balcony—

Toys—there are children here—

I remember her infamy, so safe in black and white,
in roller skates and a pinafore dress,
her chin pressed firmly down, her eyes fixed,
her hands—clasped—fingers tight—
there was no fear there, only wonder—
Who is this man? Why must he look so fierce?
Did she ever trip on the roadside,
bold as any slabs of concrete might be?

Coming back along, I bid farewell to my companions—
they are here for the ages, so they have been set—
where is she now? Does she still skate?

Gods

I was there in Ninety-Nine,
when *the giant* from the east
held *the King* at bay—
And before, that local row
decided in the real capital,
the rain-soaked mob promising,
unaware, that the south would rise again.
The amphitheater rang
as emperors watched
weapons and helmets buckle—
not men, but giants, we were told,
the pillars of society,
that must be kept at all costs,
lest the arena fall empty.
Bums must be put on seats
if civilization is to thrive.
Could Homer see or hear the shouts,
he would know that, yes,
Gods do make their own importance,
but it's the mob that allows men
to wear their cheap tunics.

Pegeen

In the good old days
we'd pull up our sleeves
and beat the fools
for tellin' stories wrong,
as easy as swattin' flies
with the Homestead—
now we're weak,
and don't say a word
when they erect
the cold steel.

Back to Boom

We are the leaf-eaters,
plastering billboards
with the familiar promise
of fast approval for dreams.

Grubs, waiting to be grown,
so we can taste the towering
steel, that was just there,
and then gone, and now back.

Cranes

Nobody knows
where they come from—
they are just there
one morning,
casting shadows
over your breakfast.
Ten years ago
we talked of everything
but honour and truth,
measuring men
by the shadows
that they cast.
Like children
with off-brand Lego,
we stacked blocks
to create solitude,
but there is no solitude
to be found
within those yellow walls.
Breakfasts have become brighter,
and quieter,
but we keep an eye
out the window,
for shadows and cracks.

Monuments

We have erected monuments
in homage to Flavian
throughout this realm,
once tall and bright,
now crumbling and smeared
in a green grime
that any power-hose
would wash away in seconds.
Vonnegut claims the flaw in humans
is that everyone builds, nobody maintains.
Look across this tract,
and see if his words are true.

Dynasties

He split the South East
to ensure her selection,
and placed his underling
as a fourth candidate
in a constituency
where they had agreed on three—
and then they knocked,
and promised that the days
of old-school politics were behind us.
In the national news
they bickered about hierarchies
instead of deficits,
council seats instead of hospital beds.
Austerity and its likes love this island,
where they can grow fat on cronyism,
and not worry about bad press occupied
by appropriately named public servants,
whose only qualification is their birth cert,
and posters capturing trained smiles
that proudly declare to passers-by—
  this is Ireland!

Rivers

You know
you're of a place,
when you comment
on the height
of the river.

Ash

She bore her bump
with pride,
but I would not lie with her,
though I had before.
The same, again,
was all she wanted,
nothing more.
Memories paint far finer portraits.
I accused her of asking the same
of other men—
but nothing more,
was all she said.
We tied portraits
to windows
so we'd not be saddened
when the mist came
up from the south.
I asked her why not me alone—
All men, alone. Nothing more.
She had more children than teeth
in that mocking jaw—
children, who just didn't know.

Petals

It was frightening in that ivory jungle—
a thousand shades of cream—the animals,
deathly still, not a twitch from skin—

Such places cause wanderers to starve—
you cannot eat these monotonous petals,
machine-wrought and worthless—

The Mob

Down in the low embankment by the ninth,
we caught glimpses of the apocalypse—
no hop-ons, that was the plea, drowned out
by the applause, *oggy oggy oggy, oi oi oi!*

Held down, he spat in his face, disgusted
to be pinned—this wasn't how boys behaved,
the mob needed a show, the mob would talk—
show their thumbs. *Oggy oggy oggy, oi oi oi!*

Nobody knew how we came to the hollow,
but there we were, telling mothers the usual,
that we'd training or detention, anything to keep
the soft women happy—innocent of our deeds.

We were men going to war, why trouble them
until we came home, teary-eyed, with scrapes
that needing mending, and stories we hoped
would be dragged out of us so we'd sleep sounder?

I really wanted to make him cry. But he pulled
a compass, waving it wildly, sensing the loss
of his bravado, he needed to be sure that the mob
would tell the history of it differently.

On quiet days we just lined the corridors, beating
the smaller fellas, as we'd been shoved and kicked
when we were new and timid, walking that passage
built of the cold white stone from sleepless nights.

Hatred rose and died without reason, even now
it makes little sense, it was just the way we were,
the way we had to be, forgetting the useful words—
all we wanted was oggy, oggy, oggy, oi, oi, oi.

Beautiful

It was as a sports bar should be—
sweet barbeque filled testosterone;
an unlikely mistake in a black dress.

The bus ran by, drawn by a chord,
as we gazed down, drawing
each other into adolescence.

They're different at home.
They don't run like that.
What's it like? *Grey. Beautiful.*

Confirmation Party

Manoeuvring through white urban off-roaders,
we watched our step, conscious of the faces
peering out, those in the know taking the chance
to brief the other onlookers on anything pertinent.
We were warned not to mention his procedure,
to feign ignorance at the new head of hair
that had sprung up on his head overnight.
Having placed our offerings on the altar,
we shuffled into a suitable space, accepted
our vessels, and settled in for the wait.
Out back, the giant bouncing castle seemed
a more suitable venue for comparing our manhood,
but it was up atop some freshly placed slabs,
the negotiation of which would have been difficult,
after the host, tightly tucked, had seen to it
that we were looked after like teens in ditches.
The talk was simple—who owed, who was owed;
there was much on the things that people did.
We were told to tell a child what to do with life,
because he was one of those that could do anything,
and so must listen to those in the know, his father's
advice soundly reified. We ate catered food with wine
marked "fine" on the label. The night ended in a bathtub—
the shower guard having given way. Who was confirmed,
neither of us can say, but we learned much about
these wonderful strangers, and the wonderful things they do.

Platform Two

In May I crossed Dublin on the Luas,
going from one station to its disconnected other—
here, stations point in only one direction.

We left Connolly with little more than a lurch,
as gently, the old Enterprise geared up
for her journey north, beyond Kilnasaggart.

Skirting the coastline, the sea was just as grey,
and the fields we came upon were green, filled
with cattle and sheep, idle and chewing.

Pulling into Dundalk, I noticed the yellow backdrops—
bus scoile—and the signs you could read twice,
hanging by a poster for Roddy Doyle's new novel.

We crossed a river or two, but little else.
I watched on Google Maps, as we overcame
the dense grey line, sketched out with precision.

A brown stain smeared the carriage window,
much to the distraught of the New Zealander
whose heart had been set on filling his Instagram.

Looking out on Newry, the sprawling mosaic
with its momentary flashes, was so familiar
that I might as well have been staring across the Glen.

As the grey line grew farther from our backs,
the signs needed reading once, and children climbed
on the bus—the livestock still enjoyed the grass.

My New Zealand friend looked disappointed—
as we came upon the rising smoke, the first thing
we saw was a provocation, pushing Roddy Doyle.

Malin Head

They posted a picture
in *The Journal*,
of the Aurora Borealis
sat atop the Milky Way—
"I can't believe this is Ireland," it read.
Far from Malin,
the site of this wonder,
there was a son emigrating,
and a daughter sleeping
under a European-funded bridge.
Malin Head is a vantage point
as good as any,
but the stars there
are a long way away.

Caricatures

They mimicked her limp,
laughing at the way she swayed—

I just had an exam, I need sleep—

They revelled, explaining designated
driver schemes meant free mixers—

I'm crawling the walls—

Nursing the throbbing, they swore,
again, never to touch another drop—

Generation Gap

Swallowed by his chesterfield, he warned
that *time will not be bested*, his heart
pinned to the lapel of his grey-tweed jacket.

We listened intently, our football shirts
half-tucked into the O'Neill's trackies
that had bellowed as we came up the drive.

Now the wind catches Hollister pyjamas,
and the rain falls on pink vests, good for
wiping black plastic ski-goggles.

At the Travelodge

They took umbrage with the other fella
getting a *free ride* because he was handy
with the small ball, passing exams
based on books he hadn't even read.
They criticised those in the Jungle,
ignorant of the modern times that dawned
while they were too occupied with lions.
With the wisdom of age I joined them,
the dawn had not been lost on me,
having been thoroughly exposed to culture.
But then I spoke with a man thrice my age,
who found it hard to listen, and see,
but pined little for his lost senses
as he stole away into his stories, supping
his quart—he was but a foot from me,
but I was the only one in that room
when Tullaroan won the first of many.
And then I remembered another story,
about a young boy in a Travelodge,
loaded up from the vending machine,
and heading back to the twin room
with change for his dad—it wasn't
that he was hungry, they'd had grown-up
steaks an hour before; there was a vending
machine in the hall, and to him,
that was fore amongst the marvels.
As the taxi brought them over the hill,
he saw, for the first time, the sprawl
he'd love, and knew that there was more
to the world than he had been told.
Enlightenment doesn't matter to boys
that have never seen vending machines
in hotels—who, years later, will retreat
to the sound of their father's snores,
waking them from dreams of chanting,
that would be even louder come September.

Two Fridges

Amid the talk
of who owed who,
he told his guests
why he had two
American-style
refrigerators—
He had spent
an absolute fortune
on one,
but the ice
wasn't dispensed
at a perfect chill,
so they
provided another,
and he kept
the dud out back,
for such occasions,
when they moved
it in for the beer,
wine, and desserts.

Uniforms

The clock would tick towards its chime,
and they'd twist like gears as the horn rang
in the deep and hollow halls—turning
like crankshafts, they'd heave, in unison,
towards the cage, their dark worksuits
marking them as disciplined pistons
in a row of six—and then they'd sink,
deep below, with their brothers,
or their sisters, to that hallowed club.
There were times when one would rise,
with coloured hair instead of a grey cap,
or legs in place of a pleated skirt—
a pierced nostril—a bearded face—
an untucked shirt—or dull shoes, unable
to reflect his light spreading across the city.
And when they rose, their brothers dragged
them back into line, so they could pound,
disciplined, with each tick and horn-blow.

Nods and Volleys

We chased the ball
so we'd feel worthy
of our ten pee pints of raza,
for which the ESB Sports Club
was so widely famed.
We basked in the glory
when luck sat the ball
so neatly on your ankle
that it dipped with grace
into the far corner.
We pass there rarely now,
and alone,
to see the grass undisturbed,
behind worn-out Coke machines,
better kept than the rusting bars
we once held up
as the champion's target—
are we so old now,
in our twenties?

Free Gaff

They gathered 'round as she took a stand
among the half empty cans and paper cups,
diligently revising their Irish declensions.

He marked her jeans as he lay on her knee,
drool seeping out the corner of his mouth—
she'd not have noticed had his friends kept shtum.

They walked under streetlamps, conspiring
like teenage congressmen, sipping a second
can as the sun peered, convinced of everything.

Be Prepared

Bí ullamh, we were taught,
as we snapped to attention under
the banner of predatory birds,
and raised our hands in unison,
chanting our thanks to the Lord,
swearing loyalty to our promises.
Our lanyards hung where badges
were carefully stitched onto sky
blue cotton—it was comfortable,
so we could string three-ply sisal
with ferocity, racking frames
for cooking pots and doorways,
as easily as we tied polished shoes.
We learned about knots and fires,
sharpened knives and pitched tents—
they were teaching us to survive,
to *be prepared* when out beyond
the realms of men, where beasts
would see to it that we were closer
to the birds than in our cold halls,
sat atop our hollow benches.
Camaraderie, that was our tenet—
this was a place for everyone,
one banner for us all to stand under,
whether at attention, or at ease,
provided our leaders approved
of the shade, and brand, of our slacks.

Walls

When we were seventeen
we took that handy trip,
across on the Stena Lynx,
to where a girl had fallen—
we had to watch
the best part dry and bored,
cursing our luck and the dead.
At Limerick junction
we drank tequila shots—
on the platform
he produced a knife
and some lime,
and sachets of salt
stuffed in deep in his bag.
We forgot our belts,
but made do with kettletops.
Heading into Rosslare
we flirted with yellow-bellied
young ones, from a distance,
egging each other on to bravery,
but none of us were brave—
there'd be years for that,
other runs to Fishguard.
Now, shops are for bread and milk,
and petrol stations
for re-filling the tank.
The empty cans lie where dropped—
those were the days,
spent sitting on walls.

Visions of Tragedy

You hardly grew
without your absent father,
but in your short time,
put down a monochrome
vision of gorgeous Tragedy
for the ages to forget.
Your unfinished sketches
could be layered atop images
of Europe's new Pana,
and as easily penned last year.

Feis Maitiú

For Br Paul O'Donovan, OFM Cap.

He would sit in stretched nylon,
breaking the darkness with his swaying head—

High pitched groans would ring out,
deepening, as pegs twisted—

Golden, the bust stood solemn, casting
disapproving stares at misplaced notes—

In the green room lay daily editions,
each one citing newer betrayals—

Acknowledging evil, he'd turn to his work,
so children could perform, and laugh, and learn.

Arrivals

Producers make sure the crew is prepped—
nice and close, get the tears—
Green shamrocks, gradated tussled hairs—
welcome home, you're looking well—
This was all carefully foretold by Finuge's finest,
reading, with pause, from those heartfelt words—
the loss of the youth of our country will create problems
in the future and it is necessary to address this now—
the exodus had given rise to a loss of *skills*,
precious *skills*, experience—*newfound confidence—*
we could use all that, and it makes for great watching—
we've got the mics, right now, up to arrivals—
                    always arrivals.

Refreshing

I scroll down, refreshing,
hoping to see your name
appear in bold—one unread—
or a ping from Whatsapp,
even an old-fashioned text—
but there is nothing.
The coffee filter stutters,
filling my workspace
with a familiar smell—
it nauseates me now,
serving only as a reminder
for delirious afternoons
spent in Cork Coffee Roasters,
scoffing Tunnock's,
flicking idly through the ads
printed on pink pages.
It is too humid here
for the month that's in it, and silent—
when I sit on the bench
by my red-brick building,
I can hear the autumn leaves
settle by my side—
they sit where you sat,
when we would laugh,
and gossip, and plan our various conquests.
We would remark on those who passed,
wondering if it were a date,
or perhaps a breakup,
arrogant in the knowledge
that we were safe from such heartache.
But now, it is just me and the leaves,
and a thumb strained from swiping,
waiting for a message that will not come.

Kodak Moment

Steps turn quicker
when drawn
by polyphonic melodies
ringing from your laptop—
yes, accept the incoming call,
with video—these days,
it's almost like being in the room.
You look nice today.
It was your hair, shorter now—
setting the trend—
and your fresh piercing, your helix—
all part of your reinvention,
your second coming, post-us.
Have you any news?
But you are tired—jaded by screens—
frustrated with my frozen portrait—
sick of verbal comfort.
Not long now.
It became our maxim,
a shallow rallying cry
we used to stay safe
in our prolonging,
but even the orchid
from your visit withered
for lack of attention.
A lot of people want to get off the island.
It was about desire, he said,
desire to see another part of the world.
Desire does not put screens between lovers,
or keep them awake,
heads torn from restlessness,
steeped in insecurity,
riddled with doubt—
where is she now,
who is she with,

why has she no expression
when we talk—is she already lost?
I should never have come here.
We're not what we were.
You say I had to,
that it was about the future,
about *prospects*.
Prospects meaning nothing when you sit,
crippled, staring blankly at a photo—
hating yourself that now,
it is all nothing more
than a Kodak moment—
scar tissue—buried
in the back of your wallet.

Progress

The Proclamation
was rolled out
as we celebrated
the centenary—
equal rights
and equal opportunities
to all its citizens—
a vision realised when,
seven generations later,
Uncle Gaybo told us
of how Clonbur
was such "a progressive town"—
a garnish of apple rings,
and immaculate roses,
and now, a new cooker.

Goblins

There's a few more lights now,
he used to say,
but they could still be counted,
five, six, high up beyond
those middle storeys,
resting like foundations,
strong and still and forgotten.
You can count the dark towers
as you trace the riverbank—
they soon turn from glass to stone,
sooth-stained bricks that cast
deep shadows before the blue night—
that way is eerie,
even for those who know the walk—
there are white streetlights
to accentuate the smoke-like air,
cold fog that dances
in the branches, framing the cliché—
are there goblins here,
I'd always wonder?
Sinister hands at work
while the porchlights fade
all along the terraces—
do they gather
between the empty factories
and boarded windows,
scavenging for loot,
picking at the construction
site around the Park,
making plans for fresh ventures?
Do they watch their towers
in the distance,
some dark, some less so?

Hy-Brasil

On clear days you could see her
peering from beyond her lessers,
Hy-Brasil, shining,
the sun drawing her from beyond the haze—
up there, it must be there;
the sharp release before the mist clears—
Even on the brightest days
you would not catch a glimpse
from this grim rock,
where progress wrecks the earth in search of gas,
pouring poison into streams;
the sound of steel undoing ancestral work;
sausage rolls and pork pies.
But the memories are still tucked away,
and the stories that he told me—
the mist has both his face and name,
but the bard, he did his work well—

You cannot rise from the devil's ladder
without biting into lotus—
the music, the beating heart,
the gushing wave—*slumber at last—*
it's there, it's all there,
towering above an ocean of rock—
there are no black rabbits or lone magicians,
only earth and stone—
and steel, brown from decades
of keeping watch over this land,
its shadow cast across the hills,
beyond the cols and into the streets,
a reminder that our knees must bend,
that the bruises on our children
may grow darker, deeper,
if from the fist of the father.
They tore it down once,
taking an axe to its stem—

but it will always rise
with roots so deep, and we should let it—
it is time that we learned lessons from blood.

I have seen her in the heart of July,
far from Porcupine and Rockall—
she is no Atlantis,
she is not a tale from the bedside,
an overzealous allegory,
but a mirage that can be touched,
a vision that can be felt—
she takes away the shadow,
leaving you trembling with clarity and nothing.
There are dead things across this island—
concrete shells that never even knew
that first breath or step;
cherished steeds rotting in ditches
like any dead beast rots—
but there are mosses and lichens too,
sucking life from rock and tree—
they cannot take this place from us,
whether high or low, rock or salt—
there, it's there, that is where the dead can't march.

James O'Sullivan has been published in numerous literary journals and anthologies, including *The SHOp*, *Southword*, *Cyphers*, and *Revival*. James includes third-place in the Gregory O'Donoghue International Poetry Prize 2016 and commendations in both the Munster Literature Centre's Fool for Poetry 2014 International Chapbook Competition and the Charles Macklin Poetry Prize 2013 amongst his honours. He has twice been shortlisted for the Fish Poetry Prize, as well as the Fish Short Story Prize 2014/15. James is also the author of *Groundwork* (Alba, 2014) and *Kneeling on the Redwood Floor* (Lapwing, 2011). He has been a guest reader at numerous venues and events, both national and international, including Ó Bhéal, the Cork Spring Poetry Festival, and the CFHSS Congress of the Humanities and Social Sciences. James, who is a lecturer at University College Cork, is the Founding Editor of New Binary Press. Further information on his work can be found at josullivan.org.